Don't Let Go!

Dr. Isaac Deas

Contributions by:

Bertha B. Deas, mother
Marsha and Ren Brighton, friends
Bryana P. Minor, sister
Tiffany Bond-Livingstone, niece
Wm. Barry Carlos, friend
Jean Carter, friend
Shirley Mann, former wife

Olmstead Publishing
United States of America

Don't Let Go!, by Dr. Isaac Deas, et al
Olmstead Publishing
olmsteadllc@usa.com
1631 Rock Springs Rd
Apopka, FL 32712-2229
Printed in the United States of America

A section in this book is provided from the book "Multiple Streams of Success: Real life stories of faith, hope, success, and overcoming adversity. Mark A Johnson, Editor, Olmstead Publishing

ISBN-13   978-1-934194-11-9 © 4th of July 2008.

Front Cover by Ray Horner, Jr. and Chris Hammett
Back Cover by Phyllis Olmstead
Copy editing by Chris Hammett and Phyllis Olmstead

ISBN-13   978-1-934194-03-4
ISBN-10   1-934194-03-4

Dr. Isaac Deas, II

 To my parents

Bertha Bryant Deas

and

Isaac Phillip Deas

My father is now deceased
but his spirit lives on in me.
It was my father who
gave me my work ethic,
my drive, and my determination.
His lessons guide me still.

My mom is my best friend.
She is the love of my life.
First, my mom taught me to
always treat a woman the way
I want a man to treat her.

Secondly, I was taught
never to depend on a woman
to do something for you
that you can do for yourself.

It was from Mom that I learned love,
compassion, and how to acheive my
dreams.

Thank you, my beloveds,
for what you both placed in me.

Table of Contents

Acknowledgements

To my mom and dad, Bertha and Isaac Deas, I thank you for showing me the way. To my beloved sister, Bryana Minor, I love you for always being there for me. My dear nieces, Alanna and Tiffany, thank you for supporting me through the hard times. To my ex-wife, Shirley J. Mann, thank you for helping me to become a man.

To my encouragers: Wm. "Boo" Barry Carlos, Newton Carroll, Ray Horner, Terry Franklin, John Alston, Cornell Ellis, Chucky Simon, Mark Johnson, Emily Lee, Jimmy Eversole, Don Buckner, Ophelia Staples, Dan Jasper, thank you guys for always being there for me.

I thank my spiritual fathers: Pastor Dan Chassie, Youth Challenge; Pastor Gary Washburn, Grace Tabernacle; Pastor Terry Mahan, The Father's House; Pastor Samuel Williams, Calvary Baptist Church; Pastor Kevin Benton, Empowering Word; Pastor Gary, Grace Tabernacle; Elder and Dr. Smalley, Macedonia Church of the Living

God; Pastor Steve Hulsey, Lake Square Presbyterian; Pastor Ken Scruggs, First Baptist-Leesburg.

To my awesome friends, I appreciate your support: Jean Carter, Marsha/Wren Brighton, Mother Dorothy Kirby, Aunt Laura Franklin, Reggie Van Simms, Ted Williams, Linda Campbell, Pat Kennedy, Pernell Mitchell, Anthony Robinson, Sammy Purvis, Dwayne Hafer, Maria Knight.

Especially, I honor and thank my Lord and Savior, Jesus Christ, who pulled the whole thing together.

Introduction

- ☑ Have you ever dug a hole so deep for yourself that you felt that there was **no way out**?
- ☑ Have you ever **disappointed** the ones you love?
- ☑ Have you ever **lost everything** that you worked for?

 I am writing this book, with the help of family and friends, to let you know that I too was that person and to send you a message of HOPE.

I had to accept the fact that I could not do it alone. I tried to, but it did not work. It took my family, my friends, and my God to pull me through.

Despite all my education, my job experience as a probation officer, my spiritual background, and being surrounded by healthy peers, nothing was able to stop me from sliding down that deep slope.

When I thought about God's grace, I made my testimony:

Jeremiah 29:11-14 (KJV)

[11] For I know the thoughts that I think toward you, saith the LORD, thoughts of peace, and not of evil, to give you an expected end.

[12] Then shall ye call upon me, and ye shall go and pray unto me, and I will hearken unto you.

[13] And ye shall seek me, and find me, when ye shall search for me with all your heart.

[14] And I will be found of you, saith the LORD: and I will turn away your captivity, and I will gather you from all the nations, and from all the places whither I have driven you, saith the LORD; and I will bring you again into the place whence I caused you to be carried away captive.

and Isaiah 43:1-5 (KJV)

[1] But now thus saith the LORD that created thee, O Jacob, and he that formed thee, O Israel, Fear not:

Dr. Isaac Deas, II

for I have redeemed thee, I have called thee by thy name; thou art mine.

²When thou passest through the waters, I will be with thee; and through the rivers, they shall not overflow thee: when thou walkest through the fire, thou shalt not be burned; neither shall the flame kindle upon thee.

³For I am the LORD thy God, the Holy One of Israel, thy Saviour: I gave Egypt for thy ransom, Ethiopia and Seba for thee.

⁴Since thou wast precious in my sight, thou hast been honourable, and I have loved thee: therefore will I give men for thee, and people for thy life.

⁵Fear not: for I am with thee: I will bring thy seed from the east, and gather thee from the west.

In compiling this book, I chose people who knew me before, during, and after the slide. These people stood by me through good and bad times. My turning point was when, with the help of Ren and Marsha Brighton, I actually admitted that I was an addict. This couple came to my house one Saturday with another friend, Pastor Carlton Giles, and stayed there almost all day until I made that declaration of helplessness.

Of course, my mother, my sister, and my niece, had to have a say. My mom is the one who prayed me through the depths of withdrawal, while my sister and niece offered moral support and encouragement. My family knew nothing about my addiction so, of course, they were in the dark. It really hurt temporarily to lose their respect, but thank God, we have strong family ties.

Ms. Jean Carter was my confidant, spiritual advisor, friend, and part of my church family at Calvary Baptist Church in South Norwalk, Connecticut. Jean never condemned or judged me, but rather loved me through the crisis.

Barry "Boo" Carlos was my main running partner when I moved to Norwalk. Barry knew everyone and introduced me to nearly all the people I met in Norwalk. He was one of the few people who visited me in jail, encouraged me, yelled at me, got angry with me, but always stood by me. Barry beat me up physically, but would not let anyone else do it.

My former wife is another story. She held out as long as she could but finally had to throw in the towel. She wasn't merely angry with me—she hated me. I had lost our home and our security. Most importantly, I lost her trust by not being honest and open. She was an awesome wife but she had her limit. I thank God that we are friends again.

The main message I want you to come away with is "God is good." He can make lemonade out of lemons by taking what the enemy meant for evil and turning it into something good.

What we do not see in ourselves—God sees. At this moment, God allows me to touch lives that I could not have reached without this past journey. Since coming to Florida, I have spoken to thousands of youth, families, couples, and individuals.

Over the past couple of years, I have traveled abroad, witnessing in Africa, France, and England, as well as throughout the United States.

If we do not have HOPE then we have nothing. If we do not have God in our lives, we have nothing. If we do not have family and friends to encourage us, we have nothing. This is my understanding of 1 Corinthians 13:1-3 (KJV):

> [1]*Though I speak with the tongues of men and of angels, and have not charity, I am become as sounding brass, or a tinkling cymbal.*
> [2]*And though I have the gift of prophecy, and understand all mysteries, and all knowledge; and though I have all faith, so that I could remove mountains, and have not charity, I am nothing.*
> [3]*And though I bestow all my goods to feed the poor, and though I give my body to be burned, and have not charity, it profiteth me nothing.*

Isaac

My Son: "The Former Drug User"

Bertha B. Deas, Mother

"Never doubt love: never question it when it comes on stage, but be happy for its entrance and do not weep when it makes its exit; for it leaves behind it the sweetest aroma of caring; a fragrance to linger the rest of your life."
Author Unknown

The first inkling we had of my son's drug use was from a girl in the neighborhood. Disbelief was my opinion of her account of having seen him "using." When his Dad and I confronted him, he vehemently denied the story—and we believed him.

Our son was no street child. He was raised by both parents in a loving home—he was obedient to us. We had prepared him, so we reasoned, to live in a world in which there were many barriers confronting black men. We told him it is a great challenge for a black man to be successful in America. You must exhibit effort, tenacity, discipline, and responsibility for your actions to meet the challenges of life. Therefore, with home training, religious training, private schooling, and his employment in the Juvenile Court system, we thought we had done a decent job of raising and preparing him for life in society.

When we realized that he had turned to drugs, it caused us grief beyond our wildest fears. We were sickened, heart broken, felt like failures; ashamed and afraid. We felt stripped of all our parenting skills. It was unthinkable for me to consider abandoning him, so I prayed to God for him day, night, and in between.

Even when children fail to live up to our expectations, we must reach out to them—we cannot afford to lose them altogether.

Bertha

Dr. Isaac Deas, II

The Ultimate Challenge

Marsha and Ren Brighton, friends

*O my people, what have I done
unto thee? and wherein have I
wearied thee? testify against me.*
Micah 6:3 (KJV)

What struck me when my husband, Ren,
a mutual friend, Carleton, and I first saw Isaac
that day was how much pain he was in—not
just physical, but also psyche. I did not know
Isaac very well. I had met him through the
Juvenile Court in Norwalk, and he had
suggested I join him on the Board of Mid-
Fairfield Child Guidance.

He was always upbeat, cheerful, and
seem to be a positive thinker (a far cry from
the hurting pup I saw at his home that day). He
had talked me into becoming a volunteer
probation office for the Norwalk Juvenile
Court. I even offered to do some typing for
him during his first attempt to apply for a

Doctorate degree. However, I did not know anything about his private life.

I was shocked when Carleton told us that Isaac was in serious trouble because of drugs. His wife had already left him, he was in danger of losing his house, and was on the verge of losing his job (frankly, since he was in charge of counseling troubled teens, I couldn't understand why they had waited so long to fire him).

We talked with his parents in West Haven and they explained that if we could get Isaac into a treatment plan that weekend, there was a chance their lawyer could get everything put on hold. So, my husband, Ren, and I went in one car and Carlton followed us to West Haven where we were determined to do a "Twelve Step" intervention.

I will not go into detail about what we said, but I do remember at one point Isaac resisted going into treatment that day because he wanted to go after the weekend. I remember him asking, "Don't you trust me?" I replied, "I trust you; I don't trust your addiction."

Finally, we were able to get Isaac to agree to enter a rehab program that weekend. For the next thirty days, we were able to breathe a collective sigh of relief. However, soon after he was released from that first program I received a call from his mother, Bertha, telling us Isaac had relapsed and was back on the streets.

After getting report after report from her about how dire his condition was, Bertha called to say Isaac had apparently hit bottom, calling her to say that he knew he needed help and was willing to go through with rehab. She explained that they had found a wonderful rehab program in Florida, and that Isaac was on his way. What a sense of relief and happiness for Isaac and his parents.

The rest is history. I do not recall the exact timeline, but some months after Isaac finished his rehab and established himself in Florida (as explained in his story in "Multiple Streams of Success"), he was scheduled to speak at his family's church in Norwalk, CT and Ren and I were invited to attend.

I find it hard to describe how we felt when we saw Isaac speak from the pulpit. It was truly a miracle—a resurrection, I felt. From having been the scrawny, sickly man he had been just a short time ago, to the vibrant, strong, vital person he had become was truly amazing. He spoke eloquently, not pulling any punches, about what he had done and what he had gone through. He made it through hell and came back.

We still keep in touch with Isaac and, of course, with Bertha, so I get all the news about the wonderful work he has been doing. His accomplishments are numerous, as are the number of people he has been able to reach and help.

Ren and I are blessed to have been part of the success story of this most amazing young man and his extraordinary story.

Marsha and Ren

Two years can make a difference!

Bryana P. Minor, Sister

> *The LORD also will be a refuge for the oppressed, a refuge in **times** of trouble.*
> Psalm 9:9 (KJV)

I am two years older than Ike. I find that your perspective is always different when you are older. For instance, it becomes your responsibility to point out the error of a younger sibling's ways. I have always felt quite comfortable in this role, sort of natural, the way it is supposed to be, the correct order of things.

We had chores. My job was to wash the dishes, my brother's job was to dry them. No dishwasher in those days—not the mechanical kind, anyway. It was here that I lectured my brother on many occasions. Standing side-by-side at the sink was my forum. Since neither of us could escape this nightly chore, I certainly had a captive audience. As the washer, I controlled the pace. The faster I washed, the faster we finished. The slower I washed…

Our dad was the disciplinarian. Sadly, all egregious behavior was reported to him by our mom. Dad did not spare the rod. It was "painful" to watch my brother receive the spankings, very "painful" indeed.

There was the spanking for losing his new shoe, just one, mind you. One lost new shoe. One "not yet paid for" shoe. One shoe so recently added to our mom's running credit with Gabe's Shoes that we still had the box.

I grieved over those spankings. It *was* as if *I was the one* being spanked—well, not really, but I was sorry nonetheless. There was the time that my brother and his best friend took the mail from neighbors' mailboxes and buried it in the big dirt piles on a nearby construction site. Some times, my brother was blamed for things done by other children, and he would not speak up for himself. He would not defend himself at all! This behavior got him (you guessed it) more spankings.

I could not take it. Thus began my lectures, while standing side-by-side at the sink. I would employ reason—"Don't walk in the water with your new shoes on." "Mommy works hard and those shoes cost a lot of money." and, the mantra, "If you're not bad, you won't get a spanking."

Truthfully, though he always listened politely, he never really committed to changing his ways. Children continued to blame him for things because he was such an easy target. He would never tattle on them. As much as I pleaded and lectured, however, the behavior continued, as did the spankings.

My brother, as it turned out, developed into a good student. He was a popular, polite, and easygoing young man with an inclusive, tolerant, and outgoing personality. What was "not to like" about that? He had friends all over our little town. Everyone knew him and he knew everyone.

College years seemed like a breeze for him. I always marveled at how it came so easily for him. I told him how I would agonize over what to say in 'blue book' essay assignments; he told me he loved that kind of testing. Being two years older I warned him not to wait until the last minute to write papers because he would bring stress on himself.

Nevertheless, he was such a prolific writer that he could turn out awesome, insightful papers in one sitting. The lecturer was becoming irrelevant.

I do not know when his drug use started. I surmised years later that it was probably during his college years. I do not think it was with college mates in dormitories because he was never a resident student. I think the drug use started during those years but with non-collegiate friends. I never realized until now that I have never asked him about that. All I know is that he was very, very good at hiding it.

A great job opportunity took him to another town in Connecticut. When he moved away, I remember being very sad. I thought he would be lonely. Quite the opposite—the boy thrived! He made tons of friends and did great on his job. I felt good that my brother had such a wide circle of friends who loved him. Later, I wondered if drugs were the common link to all these friends.

He married a great woman in what had to be the wedding of the year. Everyone was there! So many people celebrated the happiness of this upwardly mobile, likable young man. I honestly had no clue about his drug use in those days. I have often wondered if I did not suspect it because I did not want to know. (No, I do not think so. I honestly did not know.) This young man was more than holding his own—he was making it so much better for the young people in his charge. He was very, very good at hiding his addiction.

Our parents, along with two or three other families, were the first to break ground in our neighborhood when it was open, fertile land. While visiting during the construction of our home, our grandparents and our uncle saw the wisdom of buying some land, also. They sacrificed and bought a lot down the street from us. That deed passed from my grandfather to his son. My uncle paid the taxes for years and years on that piece of land.

When my brother and his new wife decided to build a house, Mom arranged for them to purchase the lot. How joyous we all were! Not only would my brother be living near us, it seemed appropriate that he would be living on the land originally purchased by our grandfather. Our dad was beyond excited and personally oversaw the construction.

On moving day, we all celebrated as they settled in. However, something was wrong. I did not know what it was, but my sister-in-law was unhappy. I heard the subcontractors were not being paid. What? My brother had a construction loan. Surely, it was just the timing of the disbursements. Rumors began to surface about money that was missing and shady friends at his house until late at night. My brother was not communicating, slept all the time and his job was in danger! My sister-in-law was crying. It could not be! However, it was. The truth came out. Drugs! He was not so good at hiding it after all.

I could not believe it. Not my 'got-it-all-together' brother. Do not worry, I will talk to him. He has listened to me in the past, right? Its okay, I will talk to him. I felt strange as I climbed the stairs. Was I afraid to talk to my own brother?

I opened the door and found him sleeping. I did not care because this was important! His wife was crying, mom was wringing her hands, and dad had shut down—speaking to no one. I did not care! "Wake up! Wake up!" He did not respond to me. That was strange. "It is me—your sister!" Still, no response. "Why are you doing this? Stop it! Don't do this to yourself. Stop it, now! Wake up!"

It sunk in that he was really in trouble when he would not or could not respond to me. I was naive about addiction and was shocked that he could not just quit. I remember feeling helpless—as if I was fighting someone or something that I could not see or touch.

Eventually, he lost his wife, he lost his home, and he lost his job. I was angry! This was a man who was loved and supported by his family! His family, especially his mom, had sacrificed for him. To me, that land represented a bequest from loving ancestors. Moreover, it all went up his nose! I was *really angry*, and I resented him. It was hard to love him at that time.

I took a course in college about addiction and learned that some of the usual signs were there all along if you knew the symptoms. I learned that addiction is a disease from which you will always be in recovery. I learned that when you communicate with an addicted person you are talking to the disease, not to the person. I learned how cunning an addicted person could be: a master of deception. It was painful to admit that this described my brother.

This experience has taught me what an awesome God we serve. If we did not get ourselves into such devastating situations, we would not know the might of our God. I tried to hold onto the belief that he would get better, even though I felt like letting go sometimes. I asked for strength, but sometimes I did not feel very strong. Nevertheless, God is strong and He is in charge. His will be done. He is faithful and loves us no, matter what. I thank God for that.

Today, my brother, two years younger than me, has become the lecturer. Our dad is resting in the arms of our God, and my brother now covers our family.

I have long since forgiven my brother and thank God for what he went through. When I stand back and watch God work, all I can say is:

Thank you. Thank You for the man he has become. Thank You for the way You use him. Thank You for giving Isaac back to us. My brother—I love him so.

Bryana

Everybody Loves Ike

Tiffany Bond-Livingstone, niece

> *Now we exhort you, brethren, warn them that are unruly, comfort the feebleminded, **support** the weak, be patient toward all men.*
> 1 Thessalonians 5:14 (KJV)

In the Beginning…

My maternal extended family is cozy. "Cozy" meaning that, although few in number, we are very committed to one another. "Committed" means that everyone is aware of everyone else's affairs. "Aware" means that we each feel that it is our right and responsibility to speculate and make recommendations regarding the on-goings of one another. This is done in a positive way—depending on your perspective.

My mother has one sibling, her "little" brother, Ike. My sister, Alanna, and I call him Ikey. I do not remember the first time that he took us for a weekend as little girls. My mother tells a story about how she was certain that her babies, especially the little one, would be unwilling to be away from her overnight. But, he scooped up Alanna, the toddler, and headed for the door with me crawling behind in my diaper and waving goodbye, as chubby legs struggled to keep up. I don't doubt that it's true. Everyone, young and old, are drawn to Ikey.

He is responsible for the nicknames that the family adapted for us: Alanna is called "Lanna Doon" and I am called "Tiffy Tuna." (This name stemmed from an impromptu song he made up one summer in Cape Cod when he came in from fishing to find me eating a tuna sandwich at the kitchen table.) While this was cute as a little girl, I did not find being named after a fish complimentary when I became a teenager.

Weekends with Ikey were a blast in our eyes. He had this huge Doberman named Omega Psi Phi, called Psi for short. The two of them were in synch in such a way that I could never make sense of it as a child. Seemingly, without making a sound, Psi would indicate his wants and needs then Ike would respond.

When driving, stop within five miles of home, Ike would suddenly open the car door, and tell Psi to get out. The massive dog would leap out and tear up the road like a horse on a foxhunt. Looking back at it now, it must have been quite unnerving for the public at large to see Psi seemingly bearing down on them at record speed. By the time we reached the house by car, the dog would be on the porch leisurely awaiting our arrival. I imagine that leash laws and other restrictions would prohibit Psi's free reign nowadays, but back then, he was better known in the community than Ikey, which says a lot.

Time spent with Ikey meant exercise. His was not the abode of the couch potato. Psi, Alanna, and I would accompany him for jogs on the beach. He would reward us with playtime in the sand for our hard work. Psi would stand sentinel with directions to "Watch the girls!" and Ikey would continue his run until he was out of sight. There were also visits to exercise parks with winding paths through the foliage. At various bends there would be instructions directing us to complete push-ups, chin-ups, or some other form of calisthenics. With wobbly arms, Alanna and I would try our best to hang on to the bars attempting to impress Ikey. Psi would circle beneath us like a shark and dart to get out of the way when we fall. The only occasions when Ikey disapproved of us was when we decided not to try at all, which seldom occurred. He could have told us to use our sand shovels to dig to China, and we would giggle at the attention we got from him and start digging.

For years, this was the status quo. Ikey would be the entertaining Santa's helper at Christmas, always arriving too late to help cook, but right on time to enliven the conversation. His sacks of gifts would be just right for everyone, with gift tags that read, "From Psi." My grandfather would joke, "That Psi is some shopper, he's got great taste!"

Then one year, when Alanna and I gleefully went for our visit with Ikey, a new face appeared. We were playing in the stands while he coached his boys in football on the field. This was especially enjoyable because of the notoriety that we received from being the coach's nieces. Boys that normally would have been taunting, or at least indifferent, acknowledged us with some of the same regard that they saved just for him. He had such a strong connection with the children he worked with, and they respected and loved him greatly.

At break time, Ikey brought over a friend for us to meet, introducing her as "Shirl." She seemed like a nice-enough woman, with a contagious laugh. Shirl's daughter's name was Tammy. I found Tammy to be satisfactory, at best. For a child three years younger than I, she was very opinionated. Why was she following us everywhere? As my suspicions about her worthiness to be in our company grew, I called over to Ikey at the sideline to ask him for some water. In a near perfect imitation, Tammy mimicked, "Ikeeeeeee, can I have some tooooo?" My shock was akin to a father walking into his den after a long day of work then finding his daughter's loafer-boyfriend propped up in his favorite recliner. Clearly, this little girl did not know that she had committed an atrocity of the worst kind. Nobody, and I mean nobody, called him Ikey except for Alanna and me. In fact, because she appeared blissfully ignorant of her status, I took it upon myself to inform her of just who did and did not get to call him "Ikey." They were "his real nieces" and not some little baby who did not know anything! I was shocked to later learn that no one else was aware of the hierarchy for Ikey's affection, not even Alanna, who had the nerve to console the intruder whom my words cut deep causing a deluge of tears. The only comfort I had was in the smug satisfaction that I got from the look of sheer terror on Tammy's face when Psi came around.

Soon, Tammy grew on me. I was never one to hold a grudge for very long (as if she had done anything wrong), and she was kind of fun for an intruder. Besides, I did not like the way it felt being on the outside. Not only had Ikey taken to her, but also so had my own big sister, who was not supposed to be shared either. It was either get to know Tammy or be relegated to the outskirts. By the time that Ikey and Shirley were married, Tammy was the cousin I had always wanted. She laughed at my silly jokes and eagerly participated in the games that Alanna invented for us. So now, Ikey had three girls, and that was cool.

The only thing better than visiting Ikey, Shirley, and Tammy in Norwalk, was when they moved closer to us. My grandparents gave them a plot of land in West Haven, down the road from us on their street. My grandfather built his house in the 1950's, and now Ikey would build one for his family. This was a group project as friends and family all pitched in. Weekends were dedicated to working on the house. When weather prohibited any work being done, we were all as sullen as the grey skies above.

Tammy and I ran excitedly through the skeleton of the house walls when the locations of future bedrooms (right across from each other) were finally framed out. However, the blueprint for the house mislabeled my domain as the "guest room." After months of work it was finally moving day! It was like a dream come true for all of us. Having Ikey's family right down the road was the beginning of the best of times, or so I thought.

Change was in the air...

My parents divorced when I was young, so most of my childhood memories of my father came from weekends and vacations that Alanna and I spent with him. About the time that Ikey and his family moved from Norwalk to West Haven (thirty minutes closer), time with my father decreased substantially. Instead of our regularly scheduled weekend visits, we saw him sporadically. When we did see him, his behavior was erratic. I was left alone in the apartment for practically the entire weekend and when he came home, he barely had enough strength to climb into bed. Waking hours found my father extremely irritable. Once Alanna was old enough to work part-time after school and on weekends, I was often left alone to weather the moods of our unpredictable father. Eventually, my father's presence became more of a scarcity. I understood this later to be symptomatic of his losing battle with addiction.

After Ikey and Shirley moved into their cozy home, my weekends became more interesting. Alanna's job, coupled with her increasing social life as a teenager, made her less accessible to me. With a sister "on the go" and a father who was incapable of devoting the quality time that he used to, an affectionate aunt, uncle, and little cousin whose company I enjoyed, came right in time. Walking down the block from my grandparents' home to Ikey's, my excitement always mounted as I approached this sunny yellow home. I always felt that the color of the house reflected the atmosphere inside. Tammy and I made the plans of children, requiring the support of the adults, but failing to consult them to seek permission, seeing no fathomable reason why we would be denied the opportunity to spend the night at one another's house.

Ikey stepped in nicely as the immediate father figure for us both, in a way. (Tammy's father was certainly involved, but he lived almost an hour away in Norwalk.) Ikey was seldom chastising, mainly because his requests of us rarely went unheeded. It was a pleasure to do as he requested because we would be rewarded with attention and praise from him, which was positively golden.

Dr. Isaac Deas, II

Shirley's contributions could not be discounted. We all agreed that he made an awesome choice in a bride. She was kind-hearted and supportive. Disagreements between them occurred, I am sure, but were never loud or obvious to onlookers. Shirley had the same desire to gather loved ones around her that Ikey did. This made for great get-togethers of friends and family. We would all sit jovially around their home as Ikey entertained everyone and Shirley prepared her famous casseroles and joined in the conversation from whatever room she was in. At night, when the guests left, Shirley would allow Tammy and me to stay up and watch movies while she served hot popcorn for us in a large silver bowl (This was the delectable, homemade, buttery popcorn made before everyone had microwave ovens!).

Ikey was a disc jockey on the side. This brought him into contact with a wide range of people and caused him to be out of the house on some weekends when I spent the night. Because of this, and because I was a child, I did not consider his absences unusual. Then one weekend, I sat playing on the floor in Tammy's room. It was a spacious and well-decorated pink room (that I envied as I imagined that a true princess would not have such a space all to herself). She confided in me how sad she was because Ikey had made several promises to take her places and he was habitually failing to show. It was not like him to pass up an opportunity to do something fun with family, so I understood why she was hurt and confused.

I began to see less of Ikey when I went to West Haven. Instead of walking down the street to his house, I was instructed to stay at my grandparents' house and Tammy would come up to see me. Times in her house became full of dread, as we knew that at any moment, the phone would ring, and an unnamed "friend" would need him and off he would go, sometimes for the rest of the weekend. This was the case on Tammy's birthday when she had friends over in the basement. We were all expecting Ikey to join us and be the life of the party, but he never showed. Shirley did her best to keep things lively, ordering pizza for everyone and serving plenty of snacks. As the evening wore down, the disappointment was evident on all of our faces.

The golden sentiment emitted by Ikey's big yellow house began to blanch as despair and fear cooled the atmosphere from the foundation to the rafters. Favored items disappeared. Promises were not kept. Disappointment became palpable. The sunshine of Shirley's smile dimmed as her inner turmoil was apparent to anyone who looked into her eyes. One day, I asked my mother if I could go see Tammy and she said that Tammy was gone. Shirley and Tammy had moved back to Norwalk and Ikey was not well. My instructions were to stay out of his house. I obeyed and refrained from going IN the house, although I did go TO the house. As I would walk past the few lots to his home, the house rose into view with all the warmth of a tomb. The lights were never on, although I am certain that Ikey was home. I would stand outside and wonder if he was in distress, or even alive, inside that house.

My grandparents did not tell me about Ikey's habits, but my mother was sick with worry for her little brother. She would frequent the flea markets where he was known to hock wares of questionable ownership and value. He would greet me with a familiar, "Hey, Tiffy Tuna!" and offer a wide smile. He would tell me of his plans to get together or to take me to see Tammy. I would become excited that things were returning to normal because if he could make plans then surely it was only a matter of time. Indeed, things would soon be back to normal for all of us, I believed. His exchange with my mother appeared mixed. He seemed grateful for her presence, then anxious for her to leave. As an adult, I can only imagine the pleading and advice one would give to a younger sibling whose life was spiraling out of control.

As time wore on, Ikey's countenance became gaunt. His physique, which was once capable of running miles at a time, appearing to rejoice in the ritual calisthenics that pushed it to new limits, took on a wiry, gangly form. What remained of the Ikey that I loved was his welcoming smile and quick mind. Even in his unwell state, he could still garner support for himself. It was not long, however, before I began to draw comparisons between the two most important men in my life—my father and my uncle. I began to wonder if this was par for the course. It was obvious to me that women were the strength of the family and the men needed help just to get by.

Eventually, my grandmother was able to encourage Ikey to seek treatment at a northern rehabilitation facility. This was good news to most. I, however, was becoming angry and more wary of Ikey. As an adolescent, I was cynical and self-righteous. There were no gray areas in my reality, only black or white. Either a person was well or they were not. Either they kept their promises or they did not. Anyone who straddled the fence seemed insincere, even deceitful.

One weekend, my mother, grandmother, and I were invited to go to the facility for a family event. The fact that Shirley and Tammy were absent proved, in my mind, that Ikey's intentions were less than earnest. Alanna made herself unavailable, much to my envy. When I saw Ikey, he looked more robust than he had in some time. He bragged of his unofficial status as spokesperson for his comrades, who apparently recognized his leadership ability and looked up to him. We received a short tour and then participated in a sharing event.

Groups of about eight to ten people were designated. Each group had at least one resident present, and a number of visitors. The family members of the resident were never in the same circle as the resident. This caused each person to be in a circle of strangers. I was the only child in my circle, and chose to portray the sulkiest mood possible for most of the discussion. I felt trapped. At first, I wanted to stay with my mother but when I looked over my shoulder at her, the painful expression of emotion on her face as she talked with others in her group frightened me. Someone in my group asked me what, if anything, I would want parents of addicts to know about how children feel. I thought for a moment and then told them that "not keeping promises hurts." The residents in the group recognized my

Dr. Isaac Deas, II

barely concealed anger and attempted to assuage me by explaining that the promises of an addict represent what they wish they could do for you. I found this to be quite self-serving and informed my group of such. In the eyes of a child, empty promises are lies. If you know you cannot live up to them, it is better to say nothing than to dangle a carrot.

Image this analogy. Once, when I was in the eighth grade, I was challenged to a race. The fact that I was wearing penny loafers that had absolutely no traction did not factor into my affirmative response. The race started and I took off up the street. I was winning by a large margin when I suddenly went into flight as my feet slipped out from under me. I landed with a thud on my back. The pain in my back was immediate, but more frightening was the sudden inability to breathe. I gasped and wheezed and tried to cry, but could not get enough air. Besides being in pain and frightened, I was later embarrassed at the spectacle I must have made of myself. Only moments before, I had victory within my reach. Next, I was sprawled out in the middle of the street with my opponents standing over me. That was the first time I had the wind knocked out of me. It took several weeks before I could participate in physical education class because of the injury to my back. Therefore, I had plenty of time to replay the scenario in my mind.

When a parent (or beloved uncle) makes an empty promise, they see this as a temporary solution to get out of hot water or an opportunity to make an unhappy child smile for a change. The child, seeing a chance at victory, greedily snatches the dangled carrot because it is a breath of fresh air in their lives. However, when the promise is not kept, reality knocks the wind out of them. How can one expect to repair a relationship later when there are numerous examples of why one cannot be trusted? In my opinion, a lack of regard would be less hurtful than to intentionally raise the hopes of the child, knowing that those hopes will soon be dashed to pieces. Of course, at that time, I could not fully articulate why the empty promise issue was such a major one for me and tears of frustration began to fall. I did not fully comprehend the source of my emotions, so I glared at the adults in the group who caused me to become so vulnerable. My attitude was as salty as my tears and no one else in the group dared to say another dismissive word to lessen the impact of broken promises. A person from each discussion circle was designated to report the salient points made to the group at large. Although no names were shared, when the topic of broken promises was raised in my circle, everyone in the room seemed to be looking at me.

As Ikey walked us out to say goodbye, he stopped and knelt before me. He told me that he loved me and asked me if I was angry with him. I had not expected this. No one else in the family had ever asked me for my thoughts on the matter before. This was Ikey— a man whom I adored and loved greatly. Normally I have great difficulty saying anything that will harm or distress others. However, drained from the recent emotional experience and not having enough energy to plaster a soothing smile on my face, I looked into his eyes and told him that I was very angry with him. Fortunately, I did not have to explain how he was supposed to be filling the void of my father instead of winding up in the same exact position. He looked into my eyes with understanding and pain registered in his. He hugged me and simply said, "I love you, Tuna." I loved him, too, but was too upset to say it at that instant.

After this experience, I was numb. I did not look forward to Ikey's completion of the rehabilitation program, as I had no expectations, positive or otherwise, for his recovery. Shortly after he left the program, my mother was again scouting the flea markets trying to catch a glimpse of him. She asked everyone if he or she had seen him, if so, how he looked.

Eventually, the yellow house went up for auction, and the few belongings that Ikey and Shirley had left were piled on the front lawn. I can only imagine the hurt and humiliation of my grandparents as the degree to which his life had unraveled became public knowledge. An unavoidable reminder on their block stood the shell of the home that the yellow house once was.

During middle school and high school, I only had sporadic contact with my father or my uncle. The occasional contacts that occurred were so disappointing to me that I began to tell people that I did not have a father saying that he died when I as six years old. I later regretted the missed opportunities, but as a child, I was hurt and embarrassed. I was weary of feeling that there was nothing that I could do to help either man to right himself in the world.

When I was around fifteen, Ikey showed up on our doorstep one evening. After talking with him in hushed tones, my mother invited him in. She allowed him to sleep in the room that was formerly my great-grandmother's my mother, as a single parent, cared for her and other family members, in between working two jobs and taking college coursework at night. (She is my personal example of strength, integrity, and righteousness.) At first, Ikey brought jubilance and entertainment to our home. He used the sometimes-scarce ingredients in our cupboard to invent tasty and filling dinners for us. Before long, however, his behavior soured the mood in our home and my mother's normally overflowing well of generosity began to dry up. Bringing him food and checking on him on the streets was one thing; the habits of an addict being portrayed in real life before her children was quite another. He eventually was asked to leave, but not before she loaded him up with blankets, a space heater, and plenty of dry goods.

With both Ikey and our father at large in the greater New Haven area, Alanna and I were always on guard when we were in public. Sightings of either caused us embarrassment and shame. We were torn by wanting to know that they were alive while fearing the reprisals of other teenagers who may have been with us. Once, Ikey showed up at my high school to request my house key. I entered the office to find him dressed in unkempt clothing, with the fume of one who spent a great deal of time outdoors. Yet, he sat with his legs crossed and head held in a regal stance as if he wore a three-piece suit. Knowing why he did not have a key to our house, I quickly gave him mine, anyway. I wanted him to leave my school before anyone else saw him. After all, he was still my Ikey, whom I was reluctant to disobey in any way. The staff raised wary eyebrows looking back and forth between us presumably attempting to connect the honor roll student/athlete, with the obviously desolate and unpredictable man before them.

Another time, while elegantly attired for her prom, Alanna was mortified when her party encountered Ikey. As always, he greeted her warmly, for family and friends were always dear to him. This sparked a rumble of whispers that left Alanna feeling deflated for the rest of the evening.

Ikey's friends, still devoted to him and praying for his recovery, admitted him into a treatment facility in Florida. My mother said that this could be better, because it was a longer program and he would be out of "his element." I was slightly more hopeful than before, but not overwhelmingly so. Thankfully, God has a way of making His plans work out, despite our skepticism. The Florida center was a miracle. Ikey was off the street, and we were all able to release the breath that we had been holding because of the fear of a late night phone call bearing grim news. Indeed, this was the turning point we all prayed for.

The road less traveled...

Addiction is like cancer, only much less respected. Everyone either knows someone in his or her family or in the family of a loved one affected by it. In its wake, families are torn apart, lives lost, and it leaves those who struggle to define themselves in social circles where addiction is not tolerated.

My uncle is an addiction survivor while my father lost his battle with addiction. What does this mean? What set them apart? Both men grew up with parents who took an active interest in their lives. At one point, both men were employed, college-educated, married homeowners. Both men were well-liked, charismatic types (and were not just brothers-in-law, but friends). One man was a Vietnam veteran, who brought escapist drug-use back with him to cope with the haunting experiences that he faced there. The other man did not turn to drugs as a means to escape what was breaking him. I do not mean to oversimplify their lives. Neither actively chose to become an addict and each one was probably astonished when realizing that it had happened to him.

When Ikey went to the treatment center in Florida, it was a very long time before we met again. Whenever Alanna and I would discuss how much we missed him, we reminded ourselves that it was good that he was somewhere safe and getting well. Eventually, the program ended, and Ikey emerged with the solemnity of the incarcerated who have been granted time with oneself in which honest assessments of one's own limitations can take place. For many, this is a time of philosophical pondering and religious declarations that lead to a new awareness. For an addict, I imagine, it is an acknowledgement that there is a higher power.

Addiction proves to even the strongest person that we are fallible and ultimately not in control of our own lives. The need to surrender to God becomes painfully clear. Done not as a passive nod, but a heart wrenching, on our knees, face in the dirt acknowledgement that we are not strong enough to survive on our own.

As adults, we may be reluctant to accept God's authority over our lives. Children, on the other hand, open up their hearts freely and without needing proof. Then again, they also readily accept Santa Claus, the Easter Bunny, and the Tooth Fairy. Still, the Bible tells us to come as children unto Him who is able to do all things. Imagine how much pain and suffering would be avoided if we all did that? Too often, we come after we have been broken by sickness, financial distress, loss, etc. Even after a commitment to God happens, the temptations of the world continue to be enchanting, and may cause a relapse into our old habits—that wrong man, gambling, abusive behaviors, drugs, etc.

In my experience, one of two phenomena occurs when an addiction survivor reconnects with loved ones after choosing to banish their substance abuse habits: either they are forever tainted or they reclaim their former status. Those who are tainted are the ones that people whisper about behind their backs. Someone might say, "Oh, I'd like for you to meet my niece Jenny, lovely girl," then in hushed tones inform, "but keep your purse near you, she's had a substance abuse problem." It is no secret to the addiction survivor. We all know when people are not treating us the same as they did before. Many family and friends openly chastise or admit their distrust since addiction demonstrates our fallible nature and loss of control. Therefore, others feel that it is their responsibility to exercise control over the addict, for their own good. How difficult it must be to battle your body constantly, denying it the addictive substance it craves, while battling the sometimes-negative perceptions of others.

For some addicts, their emergence from the cloud of addiction, and the negative actions that accompanied seeking the substance at all cost, launches them into their social setting as the returned prodigal son. After the tenuous beginning in which the friends and family seem to ask, "Are you really back for good?", the survivor is welcomed back with open arms, enjoying the privileges of being restored as a trusted member of the inner circle. This happens far less often than the former phenomena. My humble assessment is that this is related to God's work in the life of the addict as well as His work in the lives of the addict's loved ones. Ikey enjoys this second status. In fact, those closest to him must remind themselves that there was a dark period in his life.

During the Christmas of 2007, the dinner conversation, as usual, lasted much longer than the meal. My mother interrupted the amicable chatter with the introduction of a discussion topic. She wanted everyone to share what they felt their personal strengths and God-given gifts were. Then others would have an opportunity to state any additional attributes that they saw in that person. My six year old announced jubilantly that she had the gift of singing to people to make them happy (although she refuses to sing for anyone outside our family).

When it was time for Ikey to share, he paused thoughtfully before announcing that he had the gift of "gathering people together." In a moment, dozens of images came to mind as I thought how much of a gift this is. I have always felt that being around him was like being home, and it appears that others have the same impression. From the smallest children who readily follow him anywhere, to his lifelong friends that no one ever sees until Ikey comes to town and reunites everyone, all appear to naturally gravitate towards him. It is not unusual when he visits Connecticut, for the doorbell to ring at 11 p.m. and folks to come over to just sit and talk with Ikey or watch a movie on the television with him. He has a knack for making everyone feel welcome and special. There are few who would miss the opportunity to be counted in the number of his minion.

Alanna now lives in Texas with her beautiful family. While visiting her warm, "Martha Stewart-like" home during Easter week in 2008, I typed up these initial thoughts about Ikey. She and I discussed over coffee what it was like to grow up as the children of his only sibling and I contemplated the phenomena addictions. I have been reflecting on this ever since. What was it about Ikey that allowed him to become a rare, socially well-adjusted addiction survivor? We acknowledged that he was always devoted to his family and maintained a kind spirit that allowed him to act as a caretaker for others, even during the lowest points in his life. However, the greatest harm that he did to his loved ones was the harm he did to himself. Abundant are the stories of addicts who steal from elderly relatives and sell family treasures. Hurtful are the relatives who attack those who love them most with hateful words and sometimes physical assaults. None of that existed with my uncle, to my knowledge. (I guess I will have to read the rest of this book to get the full inside scoop!)

Therefore, when you get right down to it, perhaps the reason for Ikey's barely tarnished role as a leader among his peers and loved ones has less to do with our piety and more to do with his own relationship with Christ. Had God not sustained him mentally, emotionally, and spiritually throughout his ordeal with drugs, then we may all have had a more sorrowful regard for Ike as a person. There are no dark stories of violation or disrespect towards his parents or sibling. He was not that type of addict. As it stands now, there is hardly a disapproving word ever said about him (except for my mother's edict that he is from Mars, like most men). He honestly has a score or more of godchildren, devoted friends, and a family who adores him. For Ikey, the battle with addiction is still prevalent at times in the conscious decisions that he must make to maintain his structured and healthy lifestyle. The rest of us have to squint to see the storm clouds fading from his life on the distant horizon. Everybody loves Ike and he is so deserving of it.

Tiffany

Supervisor Deas

William B. (Boo) Carlos, Sr., friend

*Yea doubtless, and I count all
things but **loss** for the excellency of
the knowledge of Christ Jesus my
Lord: for whom I have suffered the
loss of all things, and do count them
but dung, that I may win Christ,*
Philippians 3:8 (KJV)

I met Ike Deas in 1977 while seeking
work after completing college. Clifton
McKnight, aka Tiki, gave me Ike's name. I
have known Clifton since childhood. He and
Ike were fraternity brothers and eventually
became trusted friends.

Tiki, knowing of my desire to work with
kids, suggested that I contact Ike because he
had been a juvenile probation officer for the
state of Connecticut for four years. I met Ike
and we soon became close friends.

I introduced him to all of my friends in
Norwalk and he then became like family. We
were all impressed with Ike because he had his

Masters degree and we were all just completing undergraduate studies. A young black man with a Master's degree was very impressive.

Ike wrote a character reference for me when I applied for a juvenile probation officer position. Ike's letter carried weight because he was well respected.

Ike taught me the ropes as a new probation officer and persuaded me to start taking classes with him towards a Master's Degree at the University of Bridgeport. This would have been Ike's second Masters and my first. While I never finished, he did.

Ike was always big on education and often advised his friends to improve ourselves. Of course, Ike went on to become the supervisor in his office and did his job extremely well (until he started experimenting with drugs).

Ike was active in his church, he coached football, he was well known in his community, and he was about to marry a wonderful young woman by the name of Shirley Bolden. I later participated in their wonderful wedding. His life seemed like it was going in the right direction. In fact, Ike had EVERYTHING going for him until some of his bad influences got the best of him and then he slid downhill fast.

He built a house a few doors down from his parents' house. He was so popular that he had his friends help build the house. Although, he had carpenters and builders on the site that were getting paid, he had such loyal friends that we all chipped in to help just because Ike asked us to. We would volunteer weekends, after work, or whenever we had free time to show up and hammer nails or hand the carpenter a piece of lumber—whatever was needed.

At the end of each day, Ike's friends would split into two groups: one set would go home, and Ike would go out with the other group. After three weekends of this, I asked him, "Where are you all going?" His response was that they were going to do drugs (crack, I think). I said, "OK, See you later."

After the construction was completed, they moved in, Shirley and Ike began having marital problems because of his drug addiction. I learned this later because I was not in touch with Ike everyday, but bits and pieces of his problem started to surface.

I received a call from a secretary in Ike's office. She knew that Ike and I were best friends and she asked me if I had seen or heard from him in the past few days. I told her no. With that answer, I got worried and asked, "What happened?"

She said, "Ike has not been to work all week, and he has not called in. We do not know where he is."

By this time, I was also a supervisor with the probation department. I immediately left work and drove to Ike's house and found him there. When I first saw Ike, I knew something was wrong because he was thin; he looked unhealthy. When I told him that his staff was looking for him, he said he was only out for two days. My response was, "Ike, you are a supervisor. Your staff is telling me that you have not called or shown up for work in the past few days."

I then told him to get dressed and took him to Yale New Haven Hospital for detoxification. I did not go into the interview with him. Once I knew that he was safe, I left and called his office. I told them that he was all right and that I had taken him to the doctor, and he would call them later.

After a few weeks passed, Ike's mother called me complaining that Ike was different. He looked like he was on drugs and he was not going to work. She asked for help. This time, I took Ike back to Yale and made sure that they got him into some type of drug rehab program. One of the secretaries suggested Youth Challenge in Florida, but I think his first placement was in Connecticut. I remember going with his family to visit him, but I cannot remember the name of the facility.

The state insurance took care of everything for Ike because they knew that he was a good person and they really wanted him back to his old self. They were willing to help in any way they could. It was a three month program (I think), and he did everything he was supposed to do. When he got out of the program, the state offered him his job back under strict circumstances. He was assigned to the Bridgeport Juvenile Court under my supervision. I opposed this decision because I felt that there was a conflict of interest. I would be the one who would recommend that he be fired if he did not show up or perform his duties.

However, he never showed up for work and he was dismissed from the state of Connecticut causing the state to cease trying to help him. He eventually ended up in jail for filling his personal car at the state gas pumps. If he had been able to pull it together, the state may have allowed him to repay the money through payment deductions from his check.

Later, I think Youth Challenge kicked in and he traveled to Florida. Ike has lived in Florida since then and is doing extremely well. He now has his Doctorate, a consulting office, and he is an associate pastor at a church.

Boo

Part of the Tapestry of My Life

Jean Carter, Friend

*A man that hath **friends** must shew himself friendly: and there is a friend that sticketh closer than a brother.*
Proverbs 18:24 (KJV)

Someone once said that individuals come into our lives for a season, purpose, or a reason, and when they have accomplished what they were supposed to do, they are gone. They went on to say that, some individuals become an intricate part of our life, and Isaac B. Deas, II has been the latter in my life.

I first saw Isaac more than 30 years ago when he visited the worship service of the Calvary Baptist Church in South Norwalk, Connecticut. A friend of his mom, Mrs. Ophelia Davis, had invited him. Isaac was impeccably dressed, his eyes twinkled when he spoke, and he displayed a warm and genuine smile. Obviously, he made an impressive entrance and turned many heads that Sunday morning.

At first, I did not engage Isaac in conversation choosing to observe him. You can learn a lot about a person when they are unaware that you are watching them. In our church, we walk around for the offering and Isaac had a walk that would make any soldier proud. He exuded confidence when he strutted around with stomach in and shoulders back. As I got to know him, I asked if he had been in the military and, to my surprise, he hadn't.

After attending our services for a while, he joined Calvary and was baptized by the late Reverend Samuel J. Williams, pastor and founder of the church. In 1979, Isaac joined the Senior Ushers Ministry. He immediately bonded with the male members and endeared himself to the females. He became very active with the ministry. Not only did he serve our church, but he also traveled with us to other church usher's anniversaries and supported our pastor at preaching engagements. Isaac was always well received and the ushers naturally gravitated to him because of his personality and winning smile. More than once I heard female ushers say, "He is such a gentleman."

During the early years at Calvary, Isaac participated in many fundraising events sponsored by the ushers including modeling in fashion shows wearing his signature hats to correspond with his suits. He also provided the music for the shows, and became a very sought after disc jockey. His love of music was evident by his vast musical library.

Isaac has an innate gift for working with kids. For fifteen years, he worked as a Supervisor of Juvenile Probation for the state of Connecticut (he and Maria Knight were the first two Black supervisors in the system). Tough, but fair, he believes he can help change negative behaviors and he gives his all to achieve this. Isaac feels a real sense of accomplishment when he is able to help one kid get back on the right track. He works with kids to set goals and holds them accountable. He believes in tough love and making kids accountable for their own actions.

Early in 1981, I confided with him about problems I was experiencing with my oldest daughter, a headstrong teenager who had all the answers. Besides normal adolescent issues, she was also dealing with my separation from her father. As her attitude grew worse, I knew that I needed professional advice.

When I approached Isaac, he did not hesitate to help. He visited our home and talked with her during his free time (which he did not have much of). He gave of himself many times to counsel her and finally a breakthrough was evident. He never told me what they talked about, nor did she. Isaac has a remarkable ability to gain the trust and respect of teenagers. My daughter was not the only child he helped during this period of his life: there were many. He has a gift that allows him to relate to all types of people. I am happy to say that the love, respect, and friendship my daughter has formed with Isaac has transcended time and distance. She is always excited when I tell her that he is coming to the area and tries to see him even if it is only for a few minutes.

It has been said that you can tell the character of a person by the way they interact with children and animals. Isaac was known for his love of animals, especially his dog, Omega Psi Phi. Psi was a beautiful Doberman, and perhaps the best-trained and disciplined dog I have ever seen. Psi would do whatever Isaac told him to do; he obeyed better than most children did. It was a beautiful sight to see Isaac riding his bike to our local beach with Psi running alongside. When he would get to a comer, Psi would stop and wait until Isaac told him it was safe to cross. This is an example of the time and energy Isaac exerts to achieve his goals.

With all the things Isaac was doing during this period of his life, he was also pursuing an advanced degree in New York. His desire to further his education exemplified how important it is to him. Work, church, social life and school clearly shows what a disciplined life he led. Through it all, he still found time to help others with their problems.

Isaac fell in love with Shirley Bolden and after a period of courtship, they married on a hot July afternoon. Hundreds of family members, fraternity brothers, friends, and well-wishers came out for this spectacular event! One would have thought that Isaac had everything he needed and had found true happiness.

Shortly after the wedding, they began to build their dream house in New Haven. Isaac told me that the land was a gift from his parents and had special meaning to him. It was during the building of this house that I began to notice small changes in him. The first thing I noticed was his absence from the fellowship. I reasoned that married life, the commute to New Haven, and the building of the house was a bit much, and he could not get to Calvary as often. Then I noticed the weight change. Isaac was fitness conscious and he had begun to add a few pounds. At first, I dismissed it as a deliberate action. Then the twinkle in his eyes dimmed and the smile we had grown to expect was not as radiant. When he spoke to us, he no longer looked us directly in the eyes.

The final change I noticed was in his appearance. He was a meticulous dresser and when he stepped out of his house, except for physical exercise, he was always dressed well.

During this time, he was unkempt and I realized that something was desperately wrong. Isaac had all the signs of someone suffering from substance abuse. I recognized this because I had seen the same pattern in my ex-husband. When I had an opportunity to confront him, he was clever in the art of avoidance. I do not know whether he realized what I wanted to talk to him about, but he stayed far away from me.

It was at a wedding reception where he was the disc jockey that my fears and suspicions were confirmed. His performance that night was disappointing, the music was dated, and his clothing was shabby. This was truly not the Isaac I had come to know, love, and to consider my friend. During one of his breaks, I approached him, looked him in the eye, and said, "I need to talk to you." He agreed, but I never saw him again until many years later.

I heard many stories that I never confirmed because it was too painful to think that this talented, bright, and vibrant young man had lost his way and turned to a life of substance abuse. He lost his position with the state; he lost his wife; he lost his home; but more importantly, he lost himself.

For several years, I inquired about him when I saw one of his friends or associates. The answer I would receive was the same—no one had seen him or knew where he was. I felt frustrated, betrayed, and helpless. I truly wanted to help him because he had helped me when I needed it the most; I wanted to repay him.

Eventually one of his friends told me that he was working in the flea market in New Haven and he was going to try to find him, but he was not able to. The only thing we could do was to keep him in prayer, as did many others. After what seemed like a thousand years, one of his closest friends told me that Isaac was finally in rehab. Tears streamed from my eyes because I knew the prayers of many had been answered.

Isaac's friends informed me of his progress. Finally, they told me he was leaving Connecticut and moving to Florida. I was sad that I would not see him, but happy that he would have a new start.

Eventually, I heard that Isaac would be sharing his story regarding drug abuse at Bethel AME Church in Norwalk. I made it a priority to attend and to see my friend again. His story of substance abuse, homelessness, loss of respect and self worth, touched the hearts of everyone in the church. Some of us wept openly but the wonderful part of his ordeal was that he truly found the Lord.

Isaac always had the "gift of gab" and you would be caught up in his delivery. Everyone was enthralled as he described the day the Lord touched him and made him whole. His words painted a picture of him being in the church praying when the sunbeam shone through the window onto him. He knew that the Lord had touched him and made him whole.

After the service, our friendship was rekindled and we have stayed in touch. What he is doing now far surpasses anything he did before his conversion. Since going to Eustis, Florida in 1993, Isaac has worked as a Staff

Behavioral Specialist for Lifestream Behavior Center, Crossroads; Adjunct Professor at Lake Sumter Community College in Leesburg, Florida; Interfaith Chaplain at Hospice of Lake and Sumter Counties in Tavares, Florida; and he serves as Associate Pastor at The Father's House Christian Fellowship in Leesburg, Florida.

Understanding the benefit of counseling, Isaac has opened two counseling centers in Florida and continues to work with troubled youth. He finds time to speak at Women's Seminars on prayer and empowerment, to conduct workshops for the school system in Lake County, Florida, State of Florida Department of Corrections, Christian Outreach Center, and Coleman Federal Corrections Institution. He also serves on the state of Florida Department of Juvenile Justice Board in Lake County.

I believe Isaac's mission is to do everything he can do to improve lives. He never forgets from whence he has come and in whom he has placed his trust. I believe that all things happen for a reason and nothing takes

God by surprise. I believe that God had to humble him so that he could use him. What better way than to strip him of all the things he held dear and bring him to his knees. Because he has been faithful, God has restored nearly everything that the devil took from him and since God is not through with Isaac, I am sure he will come through 100% better than he was.

The friendship we possess is unique. We may see each other once or twice a year and perhaps talk on the telephone occasionally, but we know that we are available in a time of need. If I need prayer, I know I can call Isaac and he will pray for me. Our friendship is filled with laughter and fun, but it is one where we have no trouble speaking truthfully to each other. A friend will not only tell you what you *want* to hear, a friend will tell you what you *need* to hear. Isaac has always been such a friend to me.

I truly love and admire Isaac for who he is and what he has become. He is an inspiration to young people because he is a living testimony of the power of God. He is an inspiration to me because I see in him the revelation of Philippians 4:13 (KJV), "I can do all things through Christ which strengtheneth me."

Jean

I Am Still Rising

This section is provided from the book "Multiple Streams of Success: Real life stories of faith, hope, success, and overcoming adversity. Mark A Johnson, Editor, Olmstead Publishing ISBN-13 978-1-934194-11-9 © 4th of July 2008.

*O LORD, by these things men live, and in all these things is the life of my spirit: so wilt thou **recover** me, and make me to live.*
Isaiah 38:16 (KJV)

The Early Years

My name is Isaac Deas. I was born 15 April 1952 in New Haven, Connecticut. My mother still lives in my very first home, designed and built by my parents. They were married 56 years. New Haven is one of the oldest and most prosperous communities in the United States; its educational institutions reflect that age and richness. It was a wonderful place in which to grow up.

A prince, I felt that I should have been denied little. However, there was a fly in the ointment: my older sister. A flourishing sibling rivalry existed between us. She kept too close an eye on me, to my way of thinking. She told

Dr. Isaac Deas, II

our parents everything, and seemed always to publicize when I was off the mark, but rarely when I got it right.

A typical boy, if there was a wrong place to be, that is where I usually was. Consequently, I received many spankings, not only from my parents, but also from the neighbors. Way back in the fifties, your neighbors cared enough to take part in your upbringing, and parents gratefully sanctioned their watchfulness. I could have done without their care and interest, of course. There were eyes everywhere. Where was justice in the world?

We were a cohesive family and we traveled a lot. Ours was an open house. There was no prejudice. We accepted people as they were. My mother owned a hair salon and later became a nurse. My father was a manager at nearby Yale University. He was a culinary graduate. Perhaps I love to cook and eat because he did! He was the strict one in the family. His messages were "Work Hard" and "Do Not Ask for Handouts." My mother was more lenient, loving and deeply caring always.

Naturally, Education with a capital E was encouraged. Both my parents always told us there is nothing that we cannot do. Education greased the wheels to get you there. "Education makes it possible." It was a family mantra. I obtained my B.A. in Social Work at Southern Connecticut State College. At the University of New Haven, I got my MA in Public Administration. At the University of Bridgeport, I got my M.A. in Counseling. I obtained both my M.A. and Doctorate in Education.

With my mother, sister and other kids in the neighborhood, I attended the Congregational Church. When I grew older, I was drawn to the Baptist services.

Growing Up

I worked hard throughout elementary and high school; consequently, I was a high-achiever in academics as well as sports. Track was my main sport; how I loved to run! All work and no play makes for a dull fellow, I believed. Mine was a party life, but I passed with A's and B's. I had many friends and very good friends at that.

Drugs? Not me….

I began smoking pot in my freshman year of college. Prior to that, I was the clean athlete. My teammates elected me captain of the track team in my senior year; I was the first black captain in the school's history. Everyone I knew smoked pot—at least, those who were "cool" smoked pot.

Outside the ivy-covered walls of my rich environment what was happening? The Vietnam War, the MLK, Jr. march, Malcolm X, Black Panthers. However, it was all Rock-N-Roll and fast cars to my cool friends and me. We were above all that.

We experimented with hash and speed, but anything else was a "drug," and that meant hands-off. One day in college, some scientist among us said, "Let's put coke in the pot and smoke it that way."

Because there were girls present and I was too cool to back out, I tried it. It was okay, but no big deal. The stakes were raised with the experimentation. This led to snorting cocaine once a week or at a concert. Then twice weekly, then three times, and so on it grew.

I was never a drinker. Perhaps I have been drunk twice in my whole life. Tequila, lemon, and salt was good, but while that was my first drunken episode, MD20-20, better known as "Mad-dog" wine, was my second and last one.

Married Life

I met my wife in church after I moved out of my parents' home to my own apartment. She was a soloist and very pretty with a nice body and very pleasing to the eye. I was immediately attracted to her. She had a three-year-old daughter from a previous marriage. Truly, she was my soul mate from the beginning. Her family was wider than mine was. She had 21 brothers and sisters by the same parents.

We had our home built to our own design. We were deeply in love with each other and life. Soon our son was born. We had it all.

I was the one the first two black supervisors for the state of Connecticut's Juvenile Division along with Maria Knight. I had been a probation officer for 3 years and a supervisor for 11 years. I was successful in my work and well respected. It was common knowledge that I was being groomed to take over the whole division. Everything was proceeding along the lines of the American Dream: I possessed a good job, a good wife, a good income, and good friends.

Fall From Grace

Someone offered to introduce me to crack.

Who, me? No, that is a Drug… and a hands-off one at that.

I refused several times over a three-month period. However, curiosity and hunger for some new thrill, gnawed at my brain. Knowing I could never be hooked, and wanting to experiment further with drugs, I finally tried crack. Promptly, my system rejected it, and I threw up. I refuse to let anything get the best of me. I was determined to beat this bodily weakness, my body's natural rejection of this toxin. I continued experimenting, playing, until my system finally broke and hungrily grabbed onto the crack abuse. In no time at all, I was hooked. Practice makes perfect...

What was going on at this time? Everything was going well: I was supervisor of probation with an excellent salary. I was blessed with a beautiful wife who loved me dearly, and truly was my best friend. We had just built a new house from scratch, lived the good life in a good neighborhood, and we both drove new cars. We were well know and enjoyed the best relationships possible with family and friends. We had two beautiful children, a girl and a boy. As heavily involved in church and community work as I was in the Juvenile Division, I remained in denial for a long time until my life was affected in major ways by the addiction. First, I was late for work, then; I did not go to work. I lost weight, did not go home some nights. I lied to my wife, my family, and my good friends.

Therefore, I mastered crack without getting sick, but still I could not go out and buy it because I was Supervisor Deas. I was above going out to get it myself. I might be seen. I might be caught. I did not want anyone to know except those who got the drug for me. This went along until people started stealing the drug from me. In addition, I did not know how to cook it up to smoke myself. I depended on others who knew how to cook it, but not all the way. After I left, they would cook it more and smoke without me, my money buying their pleasure. Not fair. Why should I subsidize the thrill of others?

The only choice I had was to get the nerve to buy it myself.

That was my ultimate downfall.

It was scary at first but it got easier. I slipped out late at night to purchase my fix, but this left my wife wondering where I was and why I was out so late. "Another woman" sounded like a better reason to me than the truth of purchasing drugs.

I never confirmed or denied that another woman was in my life. I just let her mind wander in doubt and hurt. The deceit and cruelty of that action is the embodiment of the selfishness, the "I" of the druggie.

Crack is insidious. It grabs you before you know it. However, I was still Supervisor Deas in denial. I started missing work, coming in late, with no accountability. There were 14 juvenile offices. My office was always ranked one, two, or three in productivity. Cohesive, well run, mine was the model office. When my behavior changed, everyone knew there was something wrong but me. To me everything was status quo. Who knew I was doing this? No one except the few elect, I thought. Wrong. Denial was so deep that I believed the lie.

Drugs made me desperate. To raise funds for drugs, I sold my daughter's television, camera, and bike. I sold anything in the house I could get my hands on. My wife left me, but tried to put things in storage. We both visited the house in rotation, she to put things in storage, me, to plunder and sell stuff to get my needs filled. It was a race to see who could remove our worldly goods the fastest.

I went to treatment through the job for one month, and then got high two weeks after its completion. Our home went into foreclosure. My parents were both devastated. Both of them believed in Tough Love: "We love you but you can't come home doing drugs." Father, predictably, was more strict than Mother. While she was hurt, my father was hugely disappointed, and my sister was simply angry. The whole family ached with hurt, and disappointment. I literally had it all given to me on a silver platter, and blew it, just like the Prodigal Son.

I could not go to their home, so I lived on the streets. My mom, wife, and sister used contacts to put me in jail for sixteen weeks, hoping I would lose the need for drugs while there. I got high the very day I was released. Why? I met and made friends with the drug pushers in jail. Therefore, upon release they told me where to go to get the best drugs. With the mention of their names, I was set. Crazy thinking. A roller coaster ride of drugs...

Back to the streets I went. I existed in NYC and Connecticut crack houses, or slept in cars, on park benches, in storefronts, cardboard boxes, or any other home I could find. I lied, conned, and cheated, but I was never violent or a thief. Because I had the gift of gab, I could and did talk others into doing what I wanted. Women supplied my primary needs of food, shelter, sex, and drugs. Crazy life: I was panhandling, running schemes, conning people. I knew the street life well and I was good at it. You can always make money if you think through the process. Education makes it all possible. After all, practice makes perfect.

Overdosing was a regular happening: using too much or getting bad drugs mixed with who knew what. The result was stomach cramps, followed by endless dry heaves, and then sleeping for a full day without waking up. Why? Because you are up all day and night, running your scheme. Shakes, nose running, joints hurting, you get cold then hot then cold again, then hot again, your body searching for sanity—or sanctuary from itself.

The only way to come down from being so high is to take a downer. For me, the hands-down favorite was heroin, another drug that I swore that I would never use. Repulsed by needles, I snorted it. This also makes you throw up, but the reward afterwards is a beautiful high. Alternatively, so we tell ourselves...

Things I saw while in the life: Women selling their daughters to pushers for drugs. People dead with needles still in their arms. Other junkies pulling out the needles and sticking them in their own arms. Men prostituting themselves, women, the same, me, the same. People, both men and women, beaten up for non-payment. Police selling drugs or keeping them for themselves. People being shot or stabbed. The mole people living underground. Yes, here in America.

Sometimes I felt hunger, but had no money for food. Restaurant trashcans beckoned. Outside the restaurants where the waiters knew me, I patiently waited for them to discard their unused food. Why not? They would only throw it out anyway. Occasionally, Mom would feed me if I could visit her without Dad being there. Sometimes friends provided a meal. Nevertheless, the cafes and restaurants were always dependable. My dear long-suffering wife finally began divorce proceedings. By then I was so far removed from reality, I knew nothing about it—or remembered nothing. Later, while in rehabilitation down South, someone told me I was now divorced. I felt immense sadness about letting down my beloved soul mate and friend.

One day I went to get high and God had taken the taste away. In my prayers, I asked Him to take the taste away. Two years into my addiction, He did. I called Mom and she said she had been waiting for my call. Once again God had revealed to Mom in a dream what He was about to do. Three days later, it happened. God always kept her informed about what He was going to do with me. Did she worry? Yes. Did she cry? Yes. Did God come through as He said He would? Yes. Did she ever doubt God? What do you think?

Truly, I was the Prodigal Son. My Mom prayed me through. She never gave up hope and never gave up on me. She kept that telephone line to God hot and humming on my behalf. I was not 40 years old.

Dawning of a New Day--Breaking the Spirit of Addiction

On the advice of a friend, I journeyed to Florida for rehabilitation.

"Youth Challenge" was a long-term substance abuse rehabilitation center for men aged 18 and above in Wildwood, in Central Florida. I was twenty-two months in treatment—although God had already freed me. I did well at Youth Challenge and eventually became a staff member. As such, I soon began pouring into the lives of others in the program and in the community.

The first thing I saw on my arrival was Confederate flags and trucks with shotguns in the back. This was my first trip to the South. I was shocked and not a little afraid. We had no relatives living in the South, but I had heard the stories. Was this really 1991?

Two white men pulled up, asked if I was Isaac. When I nodded, they told me to get in the truck between them. Fresh off the streets, I said "No, thanks. I'll ride in the cab in the back." I did not know where I was, or where I was going, but I watched for landmarks, just in case I had to make a break. I had no money to go back home, but I was not going to be killed willingly.

One of the most shocking facts of life in Florida in the 1990s was the blatant prejudice, still hanging around like a miasma from the swamps. With all that was going on in the world, this place was still pulling the race card.

As we pulled up to Youth Challenge, I saw other men working and walking around. Most of them looked as underfed as I was. My weight was 98 pounds at that time. Normally, I was a hefty 187 pounds. I was "half the man" I had been, literally. And, so it seemed, were my new colleagues.

Not a very modern set-up, still Youth Challenge seemed paradise to me, after living the hell of the streets of NYC. I remember feeling cold in Central Florida's November 1991. This 98-pound skeleton did not have very many clothes, and certainly no fat to keep me warm, but I made do.

Dr. Isaac Deas, II

The routine for clients here included washing and ironing our own clothes, keeping our rooms straight, tidy, and clean, and daily work both inside and outside. We were kept busy and occupied—and challenged. I immediately received the task of raking leaves, and I hated every moment of that menial work. Outside jobs included cutting grass in the rain and the scorching heat of the sun, raking leaves, pulling weeds, and in general, "tidying the garden." No matter what you did outside you always felt too hot or too cold. Of course, I wanted to help, but I wanted it on my terms. Just let me sleep (inside!) and do what I want to do and things would be great.

Wrong. Very quickly, I learned I was IN the band, and not leading it this time…

My first inside job assignment was cleaning the bathrooms. I was outraged. After all, I had three Master's degrees and was half-way through my Doctorate. The nerve of these people—giving ME that job! Did they not know who I was?

The smelly bathroom job was mine for five months. In that time, I became the best bathroom cleaner that I could be. When I cleaned it, everyone knew—it did not smell anymore. I began to take pride in my low-level job.

After that special challenge, I graduated to the kitchen with its preparing and serving of meals. This was much more acceptable, and I was soothed to my soul. I ate all I wanted. Now this was Power: people had to wait for me to serve. Cool. This is how it should be, but—the challenges continued. After meals, I still had to work outside. Bummer.

I saw many discouraged men. Some left the program and came back later. Some were rebellious and complained about everything. I just kept my complaints to myself, mumbling to God like a small boy, and silently observed the activity of the clients and staff of Youth Challenge. Because I was never caught up in anything, like game playing and web weaving, many people gravitated my way. I was educated; I helped them write letters, helped with their schoolwork. I counseled them when I needed counseling myself.

God was beginning his work in me.

Dr. Isaac Deas, II

"Promoter" was my final job at Youth Challenge, though I did not know it at the time. Standing outside stores all over Florida from Thursdays through Saturdays, I sold key-chains and tee shirts. With the gift of the gab, I was good at this. Promoters kept 10% of our gross. I became so good and made so much, that I was promoted to Head of Promotions. This meant I received 10% of everyone's gross! Cash is a great motivator.

We attended church three times per week. One grey, overcast day at early morning chapel, I was praying in a corner. God urged me to think about the people I had hurt or disappointed. As I thought of them, I began to weep.

The sun came out of the cloud for a brief moment and I could feel what I thought was the heat of the sun covering my body through the windows at the top of the room. I looked around. The sun only hit that one spot where I was praying. I could feel its heat, and I could feel the Son's hand on me. Something starting above my head descended over the whole of my body. The sensation was almost that I was wetting myself. I tingled to my toes—I felt great.

Then His Life Secret hit me powerfully: the True "Trip" is freedom through forgiveness. Wow.

God revealed to my mother three days prior what He was going to do "in three days." When I finally left the chapel for my room, the mail arrived. There was a letter from my mother. In it, she told me exactly what "would happen."

In fact, it just had.

LifeStreams: A New Beginning

After twenty-two months, in 1993 God opened a door for me at LifeStreams, an agency for Mental Health Counseling in Lake and Sumter Counties in Florida.

A friend of mine at Youth Challenge who worked his way up to went to LifeStreams first. He started working at the substance abuse division, naturally. When he heard that I had also "graduated" from YC, he invited me to come in for an oral interview. As I had recently promoted key-chains and tee shirts around

Orlando with no little success and with God in the driver's seat, I was confident in my skill level to promote myself.

I was offered the job the very day I interviewed, and was employed by LifeStreams as a counselor for seven years. The following week I began as a substance abuse counselor and worked the position for nearly a year. Beginning with 10, my caseload grew to almost 100 as the people came and went.

Because I could feel their pain, most of the clients related to me. I did not judge or disrespect them. We worked with males and females. I kept things basic and down-to-earth, but my long-range desire was to work with youth. They were my primary focus.

After a year, my supervisor allowed me to begin working with younger clients. I started with six and it grew very quickly. Soon, the Board of Education (BOE) was sending me people. As a result, other agencies began to hear about me and sent clients to work with me. There were job offers from a few, but I remained loyal to LifeStreams and its established youth program, Treatment Abuse Substance Counseling (TASC). Soon I took over that program—and began my own counseling service, Deas Consulting.

I am a self-starter. Taking the initiative is something I have done all my life. I fear no risk-taking. Many of my decisions are based on instinct, a "feeling" about the outcome of some action or someone. I am seldom wrong. Some of my colleagues really did not know how to take me, as I am not in their mold. Yes, I am definitely a team player, but if you will not play—why, I will go it alone. I never spoke of my educational background. They assumed simply that I was a drug-using "nig from the streets," now clean and trying to be productive. They never guessed those years before in my Connecticut job, I had not only run an office very successfully, but also trained others to do the same.

When I went to meetings, it was assumed that I was merely the guy from LifeStreams who liked to work with troubled youth. I liked it that way and remained quiet and humble—unless pushed too far by a

Dr. Isaac Deas, II

graceless individual. Then I would switch to assertive mode, and communicate!

My adult clients at LifeStreams were free of racial bias. Even the "good ole boy" clients respected me because of my stance: I was as non-threatening as I was non-judgmental. My mien was peaceful. How could I do my work otherwise?

They heard my message: I feel your pain, baby. I have been there. I am you and you are I.

On group days, I took the youth to Eustis Park. Merchants would often comment that I was the Pied Piper with my following queue of 16 youth. I loved these outings, loved being with them, and the "badder" they were, the better I loved them. The more dysfunctional the being, the greater the challenge, and I love a challenge. The program I started gained much notoriety and is still functioning today. Most clients today, however, come to my current practice in Tavares.

The year 2002 was a very special and blessed year for me. I began Deas Consulting as CEO and President. I became an inter-faith chaplain for Hospice of Lake and Sumter Counties (HLS). I was asked to be an Adjunct Professor at Lake Sumter Community College.

The Father's House

In 2003, The Father's House became reality.

I was a "People Person." He was a Teacher.

When I told him I was a former drug addict from New York City, I think the pastor was a bit apprehensive. The color difference was not a problem, but as he was raised in lily-white Kentucky where few People of Color lived, diversity in our cultures was of some concern. A good fit, black and white, we complemented one another. Our bond has been proven since in fire, and is as strong as steel. We work well together, albeit with occasional disagreements. He is a great teacher with an open mind and heart.

The pastor and his wife, another couple, and I met, sharing ideas about a new kind of church called The Father's House, not a dozen

Dr. Isaac Deas, II

years ago. We numbered 20 at our first service. Today we have a new church building to accommodate our 700 members, increasing with every service.

Community work is my strength and magnet. Many of our members joined the church because they heard or saw me somewhere. God has given me a gift to attract others. People are people, the color line or economics make no difference to me.

Four years after our beginning, I was ordained. The first Youth pastor, the first Singles' pastor, I also supervise the Jail and Hospital Ministry. I love preaching, teaching, encouraging and visiting the forgotten in our jails and hospitals.

Most of the counseling at the church is conducted by me. I advise the pastor and the staff when required. The pastor has blessed and encouraged me in my gifts as a community person. My heart and natural bent is for the hurting, lonely, discouraged, and dysfunctional. The pastor likes to dream and sets the vision and tone for The Father's

House. We both minister to the flock with our individual gifts.

In 2003, I was ordained as a Minister in The Father's House.

Every day I thank my God, my Father, for "raking those leaves" in my life and teaching me how to do it for myself—and how to teach others to do it for themselves.

Still Rising

A member of numerous community boards, I have won many awards for community service.

I maintain various successful and satisfying contracts with community agencies. I am blessed and proud because:

God saw fit to save me and use me for His service, my father saw me sober, and functioning before he died, my mother visits my house and witnesses the result of her prayers.

In order to leave an impact legacy practice the following:

- ☑ Remember your message is your life,

- ☑ develop and maintain a healthy family because in the end they are all you'll have,
- ☑ never underestimate the importance of education,
- ☑ keeping faith in your ability to overcome obstacles that are placed in your path,
- ☑ never turn back,
- ☑ love yourself,
- ☑ learn to work harder on yourself than your job,
- ☑ help others grow when you can, and get involved in your community.

Unexpected Life Challenges

Shirley, former wife

*Be it known unto you therefore, men and brethren, that through this man is preached unto you the **forgiveness** of sins:*
Acts 13:38 (KJV)

I had seen Ike around town taking his dog, Psi, for a walk or out for a cruise in his car. However, we were introduced by a mutual friend, Lindberg, at church. Ike was an usher and I sang in the choir. My first impressions were positive because a black man attending church every Sunday was atypical after a certain age. I was happy to see that a few good men were still around.

He had a breathtaking smile and a great physique. His chest stuck out as he walked and he commanded attention whenever he entered a room. Lastly, he was very friendly and easy to talk to—very likable.

Ike and I dated for five years, and I must say that we went places I'd never gone before like plays on Broadway, Cape Cod, the Bronx Zoo, restaurants, and other places of interest that blew my mind. I confess that I was a bit incredulous. I had not been in Connecticut long and this man wanted to spend time with me—a southern country girl from rural Arkansas.

Ike knew how to greet a lady AND how to treat a lady. He was intelligent, articulate, professional, funny, caring, sensitive, and loved to talk, a characteristic we both shared. We would talk for hours. Ike also had a vision to keep young people from going down the wrong path and he was good at it.

He proposed to me in December 1982. We only had six months to plan our wedding that took place on July 6, 1983 at my family reunion in Connecticut. Naturally, we ran short on time, but managed to pull everything together. His best man, Barry, sang at our wedding. I sang to my husband. My nephew sang and our four hundred friends and relatives had a wonderful time. Our colors were lilac and purple. The men wore white tuxedos. It was a beautiful, hot summer day and the highlight was having my parents attend my wedding because they seldom traveled.

Ike's parents gave us some property as a wedding gift, so we immediately began to build our starter dream home. At the time, we were living in Norwalk about forty-two miles from West Haven. We would drive up and do some hammering ourselves on the weekends. It was very exciting as we fulfilled our dream of moving into our first house complete with four bedrooms, three bathrooms, and a two-car garage on a half acre of land. Since Ike was back home where he grew up, he knew where to get everything that he needed.

Gradual changes began to occur. He would go out two or three nights a week, which eventually stretched out to five and six nights. Then, the red flags really started waving and warning signs became flashing red! Ike was always sniffing as if he had a cold; his nose was always running and his eyes were glassy. His lips were dry, and he was always thirsty. He began to miss days from work and church. Instead, he would sleep in, but be gone when I returned home. His close friends, Naomi and Barry started calling me to ask if he was all right because he was missing appointments and not showing up at work at all, which was very unusual for Ike. He often forgot where he put things. His appearance began to alter as he lost weight. His behavior was irrational.

Ike made my life miserable as I had no transportation, no communication, and no husband. Then our bank account and other funds began disappearing until all was gone! He depleted that in a record amount of time with his $500 a day habit. First, our bank account, then our savings disappeared within a few months. We had no income because, of course, he lost his job.

I could not believe that this was happening! I had waited so long to get married and my perfect spouse, my perfect marriage was not perfect. Something was wrong and no matter how hard I tried, I could not fix it. I felt like everything was a lie. I felt abandoned, hurt, unworthy of what was happening, lost, betrayed, upset and defiled, violated, and unclean. Nothing anyone said could take away the sting and the hurt I felt. Friends and family could not penetrate the piercing pain or make it go away. They tried with every ounce of their being, but I had to retreat and go to God in prayer. I deliberately shut everyone else out. Although I maintained cordial relationships, too much advice was pulling me in too many directions. My best shot was my Savior. To be honest, I felt like a fool. After waiting all my life for a husband, this tragic insensitive act caused so much stress and physical pain, that I became ill for the next two years. I just never felt good anymore. Every ounce of my spiritual being and bones ached. I ached spiritually and physically. I was stressed out.

Finally, Ike was compelled to seek treatment. He went for his parents, his job, his friends, and me but not for Ike. He went into a thirty-day program for all the wrong reasons, and failed to detoxify his system sufficiently. Within two hours of my picking him up from the center, Ike was "high" again and things went downhill from there.

For three years, Ike lived on the streets of New Haven, working at a flea market to support his habit. He was far removed from the real world with its reality of losing our home to foreclosure. Peering neighbors wondered what happened and were shocked to learn about this monkey, this drug that took hold of a young family and ripped us apart! We lost our home, our car, and our finances as the $500 a day drug habit, stole everything. Eventually our insurance policies were cashed in, appliances were sold, and anything else that was not nailed down.

Our home became a haven for those who had no place to go. I remember taking some time to clean the house before the foreclosure auction. A lock-box was on the door via the realtors and so you could not just walk in (or so I thought). Upon entering the house, everything seemed normal other than a few dishes in the sink, and a pot of hardened grits on the stove. Then I discovered a man sleeping in my daughter's bed unaware of my presence. "Startled" was not the word! I ran downstairs to grab a knife or pair of scissors and called our friend, Debbie, to come over and help me. She advised me to wait outside for her and I did. She arrived shortly and we went upstairs to confront this stranger sleeping in my house. Although terrified, the adrenalin was flowing. Ironically, he was more afraid than we were. To this day, I do not know who the stranger was that took comfort in my house, in my daughter's bed. He apologized and left without incident explaining that Ike told him he could sleep there as long as he wanted to. A foul, choking odor from vomit, which stained the carpet, filled the air.

My job was to clean the house and get it ready to sell. What a mess! Ike, with his traffic of people, made for a very dirty house. White kitchen floors looked black and gray, the carpet was dirty, boxes were torn open so objects could be sold, and everything was in a shambles. That Wednesday, Thursday, and Friday were spent mopping, dusting, vacuuming, washing walls, cabinets, and everything in sight to prepare the realtors for a walkthrough and provide prospective buyers with a selling point.

Dr. Isaac Deas, II

Nothing made sense: I was lost in a world that did not deserve me. I had not done anything to create this monster. Why was I left to clean and straighten up in order to "sell our home" and try to make good on the three mortgages Ike had?

This is a part of my life that I will never forget and to pen it on paper means reliving it in my mind, which at times has been overwhelming. I have had to let the words flow when I could write with much more ease. (Isn't it ironic how life takes you around in circles?) Who would have ever thought anyone would be reading my words—my true version of what happened no matter how painful it was to write—even though I am okay with writing. Old feelings are conjured up and they peak with some degree of anger, but not enough anger to slide back into feeling sorry for myself. I am grateful to God for His mercy and His grace.

I did not just jump up and divorce my husband. As uncomfortable as I was and sure that things were truly bad, I prayed for an answer. Most sensible people do not want to just walk out on their marriage even in troubling times. I chose the latter because of my relationship with God. I joined a church at the age of twelve and have been active ever since. My walk with Christ and my connection with God principled me to pray for my marriage. I wanted, even needed, to hear from Heaven: I needed to know what to do.

Six months later, God spoke to me and revealed to me that this was not the life He had planned for me. In an audible voice one Saturday morning, the Lord spoke clearly and told me to pack my bags and move. I called my pastor and his wife and my sister, Joyce. They came and helped me to pack and leave. Shortly thereafter, I filed for divorce, not really sure about anything except that I was hurting and Ike was gone. His life consisted of taking care of his habit; making sure, he could get his next fix. He never stopped the downward spiral. I remember getting a call from my mother-in-law telling me that Ike's grandmother (such a beautiful Spirit-filled person) had passed away. I tried to ensure that Ike attended the home-going service that cold February morning, however, he never showed. That even hurt me, as I know it was a disappointment for his parents, especially his Dad. He was in a world totally oblivious to reality at the time. Nothing registered, including the death of this person whom Ike loved very much and not even the divorce that had crushed my world.

My family, though supportive, were saddened by the fact that I was experiencing this thing called "divorce." I know they were praying for me and I could feel their prayers and see their concern for my well-being and my future. They did not stand back and watch me suffer. They called often, they came by, and they were financially and spiritually supportive. I was in a place that only God could move me out of. Until then, I was pretty quiet and reserved. My circumstances would not allow me to feel much joy. Most of the time, I felt only hurt and pain. Friends are few, but Barry and Shirley, Jimmy and Linda, Newton and Rena, John and Debbie, Chuck and Georgia and others did what friends do. They helped me through my moments as best as they could and as I would allow.

Ike's true friends were all gravely concerned about how to help Ike without enabling his drug habit, which was also my greatest concern. Whenever they called me for advice, I suggested that they feed him right then, and give him no more than five or ten dollars. I didn't want anyone contributing to his drug addiction.

My answer was always to pray without ceasing for God to protect him while in that state and to deliver him from this evil bondage. He needed to come to the place of awareness that he needed help. It took three years of wandering the streets before he hit rock bottom. One afternoon he showed up at his parent's house seeking help.

I vividly remember a phone call that I received from Ike's best friend, Barry, regarding the fulfillment of a dream that Mrs. Deas had shared with him about Ike's recovery. That was a happy day! Ike was off the streets and seeking help. A few days later, Ike called to let me know that he was going away to get the help that he needed.

The forgiveness process began that day for me. However, it took about ten years for me to forgive him totally and to hold no malice. As long as I harbored hatred in my heart, peace could not abound. During this time, my hatred for my husband festered. Approximately six more years passed; as I grew fearful of every call I would receive from Ike. At this point, we were communicating to a degree, however not always pleasantly as I was very defensive. I had mixed emotions about talking to him wondering, "Why does he want to talk to me now, after destroying my life? What more could he want from me?"

All together, it took about ten years for me to forgive him. It was not that I had not prayed: it was that I had not let go. Eventually, a local minister/pastor who was a friend of Ike called me and asked my permission for Ike to come back to Norwalk to speak and mend all the broken relationships that hung in the balance. With mixed emotions and prayer, I agreed that Ike should be allowed to come and speak at Bethel AME Church in Norwalk. No one knew what I was feeling. I was going to see this person I was once married to, for the first time, speaking from a pulpit. Thoughts of fear, pressure, and trepidation occupied my mind as I began to ponder the outcome. Just the thought of seeing him caused my palms to sweat, my heart to race, and my legs to become heavy and general discomfort. Actually, I was a total wreck.

I remarried in 1999. My wonderful husband, Joe, and I live in Norwalk with our families and grandchildren. We love the Lord, our Savior, and all our praises are due Him.

My ultimate prayer was for Isaac not to end up dead on the streets or locked up in jail, but that he would rise above that demon that was trying so hard to win his soul and be a force that he could not live without.

Throughout this entire chapter in my life, I did a lot of praying, and certain scriptures were very helpful and effective in difficult moments. All I could do was lean on the Lord because I had no strength of my own.

Proverbs 3:5-6 (KJV):

5Trust in the LORD with all thine heart; and lean not unto thine own understanding.

Dr. Isaac Deas, II

⁶In all thy ways acknowledge him, and he shall direct thy paths.

Psalm 46:1 (KJV):

¹God is our refuge and strength, a very present help in trouble.

James 1:2-4 (KJV):

²My brethren, count it all joy when ye fall into divers temptations;
³Knowing this, that the trying of your faith worketh patience.
⁴But let patience have her perfect work, that ye may be perfect and entire, wanting nothing.

James 5:13,16b (KJV):

¹³Is any among you afflicted? let him pray. Is any merry? let him sing psalms. ¹⁶ᵇThe effectual fervent prayer of a righteous man availeth much.

Psalm 121 (KJV):

¹I will lift up mine eyes unto the hills, from whence cometh my help.
²My help cometh from the LORD, which made heaven and earth.
³He will not suffer thy foot to be moved: he that keepeth thee will not slumber.

⁴Behold, he that keepeth Israel shall neither slumber nor sleep.

⁵The LORD is thy keeper: the LORD is thy shade upon thy right hand.

⁶The sun shall not smite thee by day, nor the moon by night.

⁷The LORD shall preserve thee from all evil: he shall preserve thy soul.

⁸The LORD shall preserve thy going out and thy coming in from this time forth, and even for evermore.

I am so grateful to God that He allowed me to see this dramatic recovery and deliverance of "My Friend, Ike." God allowed us to become friends again. It took some doing; it did not happen overnight. Actually, it took years and involved many long conversations to work through past problems that remained. In time, things mellow and they do not seem as large anymore. Everyone can change with the help of our Lord and Savior, Jesus Christ, and to God be the glory for the great things He has done.

My prayer is that God will continue to do great things and to open many more doors, to close doors that need closing, and bless Ike wherever he may go. I pray, also, that He would speak to those who are searching for a better way, a new life with God.

This is a true account of how Ike's drug addiction affected me as his wife. Although it has been painful to tell it, I believe that it will help others to know that, with God's help, I was able to make it through the painful ordeal. I have been able to forgive my ex-husband and to find healing and happiness. I never could have made it without the Lord on my side. Even when I did not give Him the praise, honor, and glory, He protected and sheltered me through this devastating storm. I am so thankful for the complete deliverance from any ill feelings toward Ike even as I have recounted these facts. It is so wonderful to be free! Praise the Lord!

There are no perfect relationships; some are good solid ones and others are bad, violent ones. Wherever we are in our relationships, we need to continue to pray for God's will to be done. Although things do not always work out the way that we want them to, God will continue to work in our lives. Even if those we love should abandon us, He will not let go. I believe that God has used these trials to help me to become a better person. I have not always been as strong as I am today, or as connected to God. I have always loved God and respected His authority.

> *"Time is filled with swift transition*
> *Naught of earth unmoved can stall*
> *Build your hopes on things eternal*
> *Hold to God's unchanging Hand."*
> ⁓Jennie Wilson, Public Domain

That is what I have done, and I will continue to do. ***Don't let go!***

Shirley

Citations

Biography

Dr. Isaac Deas was born in New Haven, Connecticut. He is the Interfaith Chaplain of Hospice, Lake and Sumter County, Adjunct Professor for Lake-Sumter Community College, Foundation Board member of Lake Sumter Community College, Guardian Ad litem, Lake County and Board of Directors for the YMCA. Dr. Deas has a bachelors' degree in Social Work from the University of New Haven. He has three Masters' degrees: Public Administration, University of Connecticut; Counseling, University of New Haven; and Education from Columbia University. He has a Doctorate of Education from Columbia University.

Dr. Deas is the President and CEO of Deas Consulting and serves as Assistant Pastor at The Fathers Houses Christian Center, Leesburg, Florida.

Contact: ideas2@comcast.net

10592207R00069

Made in the USA
Charleston, SC
16 December 2011